A First Stamp Album

Guide to Basics of Discovering, Recognizing and Collecting Stamps for Beginners

Copyright © 2020

All rights reserved.

DEDICATION

The author and publisher have provided this e-book to you for your personal use only. You may not make this e-book publicly available in any way. Copyright infringement is against the law. If you believe the copy of this e-book you are reading infringes on the author's copyright, please notify the publisher at: https://us.macmillan.com/piracy

Contents

A First Stamp Album for Beginners 1

Fun Facts about Stamp Collecting 16

Some type of stamps 23

60 Million Stamp Collectors 50

The most expensive stamps in the world 52

First step for beginners

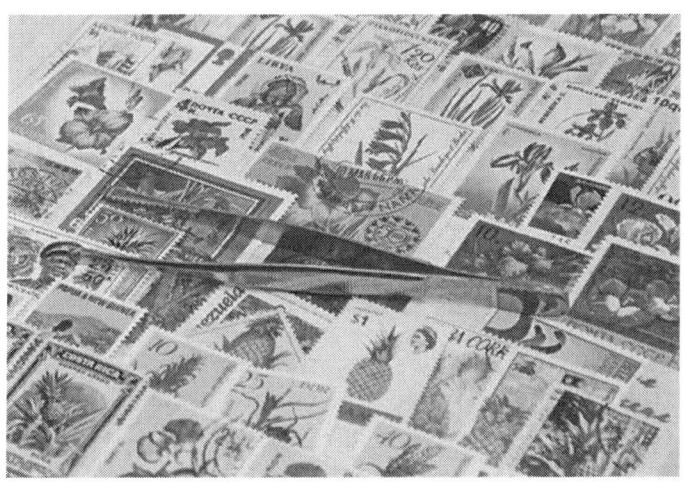

Stamp collecting is a fulfilling hobby with very few rules, but it's actually much more than that. To many stamp collectors, it's a way to explore the world, its many different countries, their diverse history, beautiful artwork and colourful cultures.

You don't have to buy expensive equipment to enjoy this hobby. Some simple stamp collecting accessories will serve you well.

Before getting started, choose a topic or area of interest that you'd like to collect. If you're unsure what to choose, take a look at our in-depth Beginner's Guide to Stamp Collecting to find out more.

Once you've done that, it's time to invest in some basic stamp collecting equipment to get you started. Hopefully, the following information will offer some useful guidance.

Basic stamp collecting equipment you may want to buy

As is the case with any collecting hobby, the equipment you'll need will depend largely on how much you intend to specialise in your chosen subject.

Obviously, you'll need some stamps to get started, but it makes sense to spend more on stamps and a lot less on equipment than vice versa. The basic equipment we recommend includes:

A pair of stamp tongs or tweezers: Tongs are essential for every stamp collector because handling stamps with your fingers can cause damage and deterioration due to the natural oils in our skin. Start with 'spade-end' tongs rather than 'pointed' ones (costing no more than £10) and once you're used to handling stamps with them, you can then find a style which suits you best.

Magnifying glass: Most collectors like to look closely at their stamps, but don't be tempted to go for anything more than x10 magnification (available for around £20) or you won't be able to see your stamp's design in context.

Perforation guide: A perforation gauge is useful to help you measure the number of perforations in a defined space, which may be the only difference between two stamps which are otherwise identical. The Gibbons Instanta can measure perforations to within a decimal point and is the most popular gauge used by collectors and dealers.

Watermark detector fluid: There's no need to buy an expensive electronic device, good old-fashioned 'watermark fluid' and a watermark tray (which usually cost less than £10) will quickly help your watermark to be become visible.

Stamp albums: Opting for a loose-leaf book or ring binder will be sufficient to store your stamps until you've built up a collection that warrants an investment in more expensive albums. These are affordable (usually less than £5) and allow you to rearrange your collection easily, if required.

Colour guide: A useful tool to have if you want to tell the difference between stamps which are similar in appearance, but slightly different in shade - which can have a big influence on its overall worth.

Hinges: The small gummed strip that's used to fix a stamp to the page of an album is called a hinge. You'll need some of these to arrange your stamps neatly.

An atlas or map: If you decide to collect stamps which are from a specific country, you'll need one of these if you want to know where it is in the world - or you could use the internet if that's easier.

A stamp identification book: Specialist reference books and stamp catalogues will help you to identify each stamp and tell you more about their background, such as how it was printed and the date of issue. Gibbons publish the most used catalogue in the UK, with Yvert and Tellier doing likewise in France and Michel in Germany. Collectors of stamps from the United States will need to use the Scott Specialized Catalogue. Well-stocked major libraries usually have a wide range of philatelic books that you can access or borrow.

Getting started – acquiring your stamps

The traditional way to begin stamp collecting as a hobby is by acquiring used items on cards and envelopes.

Buying 'kiloware' stamps that are unsorted and sold according to their weight, is another good way to approach stamp collecting for beginners. Acquiring large packets of stamps or 'stamp bags' that have been sorted is also an option.

Sorting these into countries of origin can be time consuming, but it is also interesting and tremendously exciting.

Although auction houses tend to sell items of higher value it is also possible to buy relatively inexpensive mixed lots at Warwick & Warwick sales. You may also buy items at stamp fairs, jumble sales, online trading sites, charity shops and from dealers.

Regardless of how you choose to acquire your stamps, there are affordable avenues available to suit every budget.

Sorting and soaking your stamps

Don't attempt to remove a stamp from an envelope or its paper backing by pulling it as this will cause irreparable damage. Use a pair of sharp scissors to trim the paper (about 2cms around it) ready to be soaked.

It's much easier to handle stamps when they're attached to an envelope and it makes more sense to sort them before you soak them, which will make them delicate.

Because soaking stamps is quite time consuming, sorting at this stage will ensure you don't waste time on stamps you don't want or need.

How to soak stamps:

1. Pour some clean warm water into a bowl and float each stamp (with the design facing upwards) on the surface.

2. Float as many stamps as you can accommodate at any one time.

3. Leave for 10 to 15 minutes so the water can impregnate the gum which is making it stick to the paper.

4. Use your fingers to gently peel the stamp away from the paper. If it does not come away easily, leave to soak for another five minutes before trying again.

Proceed with caution!

Immersing some stamps in water will increase the chances of the ink running so proceed with caution.

Colours can also run from the envelopes or paper to which the stamps are affixed. Soak items like this separately so you do not run the risk of discolouring other items.

If you do see the ink running from a stamp or its backing paper during the soaking process, remove the item from the water immediately and replace the water to reduce the risk of staining other stamps.

When you begin stamp collecting, it's important to stay with your items when soaking them so that you can react if necessary. As you gain in experience, you'll learn exactly how long each stamp needs to be soaked.

Stamps damage easily when they are wet or damp. Do not use tweezers or stamp tongs at this stage or you could ruin them. If you peel a stamp away from its backing paper and there is still some gum on the back, try to remove it using a soft wet brush.

Soaking water can quickly become sticky or clouded with gum adhesive and it's a good idea to change it for every batch of stamps.

How to dry stamps:

1. After their final soaking, use your fingers to carefully lay them flat (with the design face up) on a clean and dry piece of kitchen paper. Make sure the stamps are not touching each other.

2. Use another piece of kitchen paper to cover the wet stamps and gently press on them to blot away any excess water. Don't use old newspapers to dry wet stamps as the ink can transfer onto the front or back of the stamp and ruin it.

3. Once all your stamps are laid out, cover with a normal piece of paper and sandwich in between some heavy books to flatten them as they dry.

4. Leave for between half an hour to an hour, carefully remove them and leave to 'air' until completely dry, usually for 3 to 4 hours. They are now ready to mount in an album.

5. Never attempt to speed up the drying by placing stamps on a hot radiator or in sunlight because they'll curl and become damaged.

How to find a watermark

Finding a watermark can often be done simply by holding a stamp up to a strong light source. But if you need to examine a stamp in more detail, the best way to do it is by using watermark fluid and a watermark tray.

1. Use enough non-toxic watermark detector fluid to thinly cover the bottom of your tray.

2. Place the stamp design-down in the tray and the watermark should become visible almost instantly.

3. Although you can use watermark detector fluid on 'mint' and used stamps, it's a good idea to experiment on cheap stamps first. A good

fluid should not affect the gum and will usually dry quickly afterwards.

4. As a precaution, only use watermark fluid in a well-ventilated area and replace the lid immediately after use to prevent evaporation.

Mounting and displaying your stamps

Learning the art of mounting stamps is important and there are two main ways to do it that are accepted by collectors:

Stamp hinges

Ideal for used stamps which have been mounted before, stamp hinges are a small rectangular piece of folded glassine paper with gum on the outside. Made from acid-free paper, you can attach the shorter side of the hinge to the back of a stamp by licking and sticking it close to the stamp's upper edge. Lick and stick the longer side of the hinge to place it on your album page, with the stamp design facing upwards.

Pros: A traditional option, they are inexpensive and cost about £2-3 for 1,000. When completely dry, a good stamp hinge can be peeled away to allow you to inspect its back or change its position in your album.

Cons: Unsuitable for stamps with 'full original gum' or no evidence of a previous hinge. They must not be removed unless they are 100 per cent dry or damage can be caused to the stamp and the album. Only lightly moisten with a slight touch of the tongue to avoid the risk of gum damage on a stamp.

Stamp mounts

Perfect for unused stamps with full original gum, these small plastic pockets actually hold the stamps 'unmounted' within them so they can be placed in an album without affecting their gum. Hinge-less mounts do come pre-gummed, but collectors often prefer to use stamp hinges to attach them to their album as it's easier to reorder them later on.

Pros: Highly recommended for 'mint' unused stamps with undisturbed original gum because they'll remain completely protected inside a plastic mount.

Cons: A much more expensive way to attach stamps to an album's pages. Although they are available in various sizes, they still need cutting to accommodate a stamp's exact width which is time-consuming.

Alternative products

As well as the two traditional stamp mounting methods mentioned above, there are several products available that will help mount your stamp in much less time.

Stock-books: Used by stamp dealers, stockbooks allow you to store your stamps beautifully without taking up a lot of your time. Each page has several horizontal rows made from thin strips of film to form long pockets in which to place your stamps side by side. Ideal for saving duplicate items, but much more expensive than stamp hinges or mounts.

Hinge-less albums: Similar to a traditional photo album with transparent plastic pockets that are exactly the right size for storing stamps. Simply use you stamp tongs to insert your stamps into the pockets provided.

Cover albums: Covers are an envelope or postal item which normally bear an example of a stamp in use. Some collectors like them because they can show unusual postmarks. Cover albums allow them to be mounted on blank pages, using either gummed photograph corners or specially designed plastic sleeves.

Learn more, start stamp collecting today!

There are now a wide variety of stamp collecting resources available online, including forums for collectors and dealers.

A hobby which is not bound by age limits or ability, it's easy to make friends with likeminded people who share your love of collecting.

Once you have mastered the basics and selected a chosen area of interest, your hunt for stamps will know no bounds.

Should you ever come to acquire an item which you think might be rare or valuable, we'll be more than happy to provide an accurate philatelic valuation – simply get in touch with our experts to arrange a free consultation.

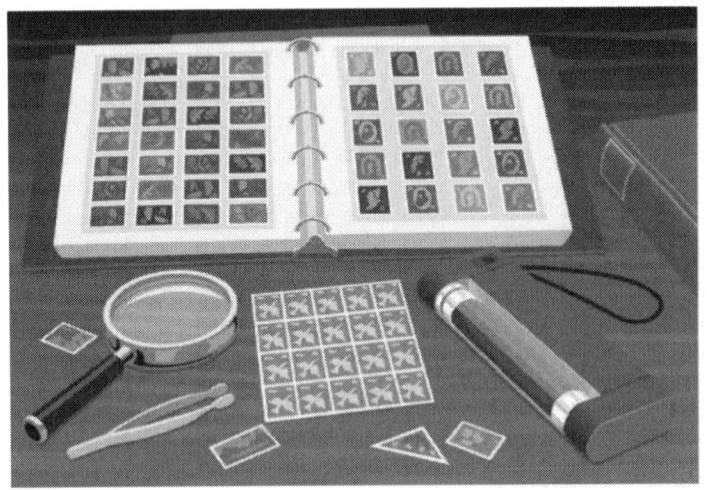

Fun Facts about Stamp Collecting

FONT SIZE

In the age of modern technology, the idea that a remnant of a popular mode of communication from the not-so-distant past would be popular might seem far-fetched. However, according to StampWorld, stamp collecting is in the midst of a rebirth that began in 2005 and is still going strong. The following are some stamp-related facts that might compel even more people to begin collecting stamps.

- Congress authorized United States postage stamps on March 3, 1847, and the first general issue postage stamps went on sale in

New York City on July 1, 1847. A five-cent stamp featured Benjamin Franklin, while a ten-cent stamp depicted George Washington. The province of Canada began issuing stamps on April 23, 1851. The first stamp in Canada depicted a beaver.

- Postage stamps did not initially come with an adhesive back. People needed to use their own glue or paste to keep the stamp on. Some sewed them on.

- An estimated 20 million people collect stamps in America. Philately is the study and collection of stamps and is considered the world's oldest formal collecting hobby.

- Products were once advertised on the back of three-cent stamps in the United States.

- Great Britain was the first country to issue stamps, though their stamps do not feature the country's name printed on them.

- Stamp collecting, not unlike numismatics (coin collecting), is a hobby in which errors are a cause for celebration among collectors.
- Graphic designers, artists and photographers are involved in the production of new stamp designs. Old stamps were printed using an engraving process.

A First Stamp Album

- The first stamp collector is believed to be John Bourke, Receiver-General of Stamp Duties in Ireland.
- The "Inverted Jenny" stamp is one of the world's rarest stamps. These stamps were produced in 1918 with an airplane printed upside down.
- The most popular U.S. postage stamp design was a 1993 stamp featuring an image of Elvis Presley.
- Aviator Amelia Earhart, actor/comedian Charlie Chaplin, Queen Elizabeth II, President Franklin D. Roosevelt, and legendary musician John Lennon are some famous people who collected stamps.

- Mailing a first-class letter in the United States costs 46 cents for up to one ounce. A single stamp for Canada Post (up to 30 g) costs $1.00.

Some type of stamps

1. A Stamp with a Chocolate Flavor

In 2013, Belgium decided to print half a million chocolate-flavored stamps. They have various chocolate images and as you feast your eyes on the vivid life-like prints, you'll notice the distinct fragrance of cocoa!

The team that graced humanity with this irresistible stamp collection wasn't solely Belgian. There were contributions by other experts from Germany, the Netherlands, and Switzerland.

The delicious stamps were issued to celebrate the chocolatiers of Belgium and their unparalleled sweet innovations.

2. A Stamp Without a Country Name

The very first postage stamp appeared in 1840. It was nicknamed 'the Penny Black', and it was sufficient to send a half-ounce package.

Before that stamp, the sender didn't pay anything for dispatching mail, and it was up to the postal services to collect the fees from the recipient. You must've noticed the potential complications with that system.

That's how the English stamp came into the world without a country name printed on it. This is still the case, and English stamps are identifiable primarily by their royal cameos.

When you're the first to create something, you get to enjoy such privileges.

3. The Most Popular Stamp in the USA

There's a list of the most popular stamps in the USA. These were generally issued to commemorate people, places, or events.

The spread and popularity of some of these stamps are staggering! Naturally, the response is related to the popularity of the face on the stamp.

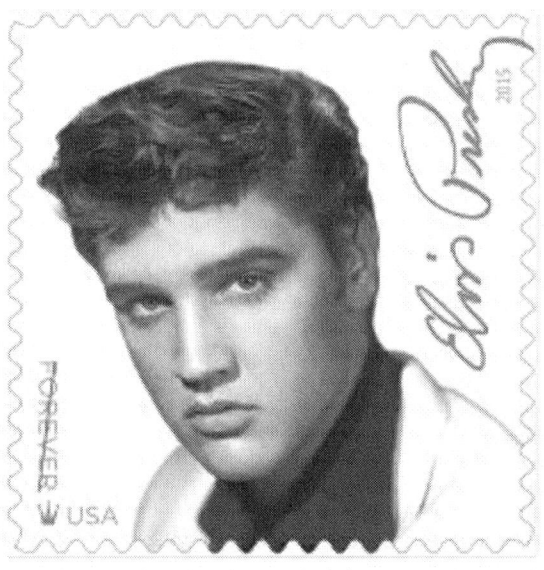

The highest entry on this list is the Elvis Presley stamp, which was issued in 1993. Until a few years ago, 124 million copies were saved.

The design probably has much to do with that success. It's bright, vibrant, bold, and so Elvis!

4. The Wonders of America Collection Goes Big

The wonders of America collection is among the stamps that sold millions of copies and were easily recognized in pop culture.

It consists of forty mega things. Some are natural sights, and others are high achievements. The common factor between all of these items is their being the biggest, tallest, largest, or similarly larger-than-life descriptions.

5. Superhero or Sci-Fi Stamps

This may or may not come as a surprise to you, but the Marvel heroes stamp collection of 2006 is among the best-selling stamps of all time.

It's a group of 10 Marvel characters, including Ironman, Hulk, Thor, Captain America, and the amazing Dr. Strange.

The Star Wars collection is a close successor to the Marvel collection, and it came out in the following year, 2007. It had 15 stamps featuring Darth Vader, Luke Skywalker, and master Yoda, among other icons.

6. Floral Stamps Are a Total Favorite!

In 1992, a North American wildflower commemorative stamp collection reached 11 million in sold and saved copies. There are 50 pretty flowers in this collection, all of them highly valued.

So what does that say about popularity and good taste? Pretty much! People celebrate many things, and they might favor some themes more than others, but natural beauty is forever.

7. The Most Expensive Stamp in the World

The most valuable stamp in the whole world was worth 1 cent when it was first issued in 1856. The British Guiana 1 cent magenta reached about $9.5 million in 2014 when Stuart Weitzman acquired it.

8. The First Non-Royal Face on a British Stamp

British stamps constantly featured kings and queens on the stamps. When something like that goes on for decades, it becomes a tradition. Until someone breaks it!

The first man to crash the party deserved an appearance, and his presence was hugely applauded worldwide, so who owns the mystery cameo?

Yes, you guessed right! Shakespeare earned his spot. In 1964, the world-famous face decorated a stamp commemorating his 400th anniversary.

At first, the Post Office claimed that they were celebrating the festival, not the man, but later on, the royals-only tradition loosened up.

Shakespeare appeared again and again in the world of stamps. Hamlet and the skull depiction were especial favorites for stamp designers and collectors alike.

9. When the Simpsons Became a Bestseller and a Flop

The Simpsons stamp collection came out in 2009 and featured four designs, the one everyone loved had Homer, Marge, Bart, and Lisa together in one immortalizing family photo.

It sold about 318 million copies, which makes it a huge hit in the world of stamps. It's considered a flop though!

The USPS had printed around a billion Simpsons stamps, which is a bit of an over projection! This optimistic estimate caused a loss of around $1.2 million.

The moral of the story is that success and failure quite often walk hand in hand!

10. The Elvis Stamp in Public Debate

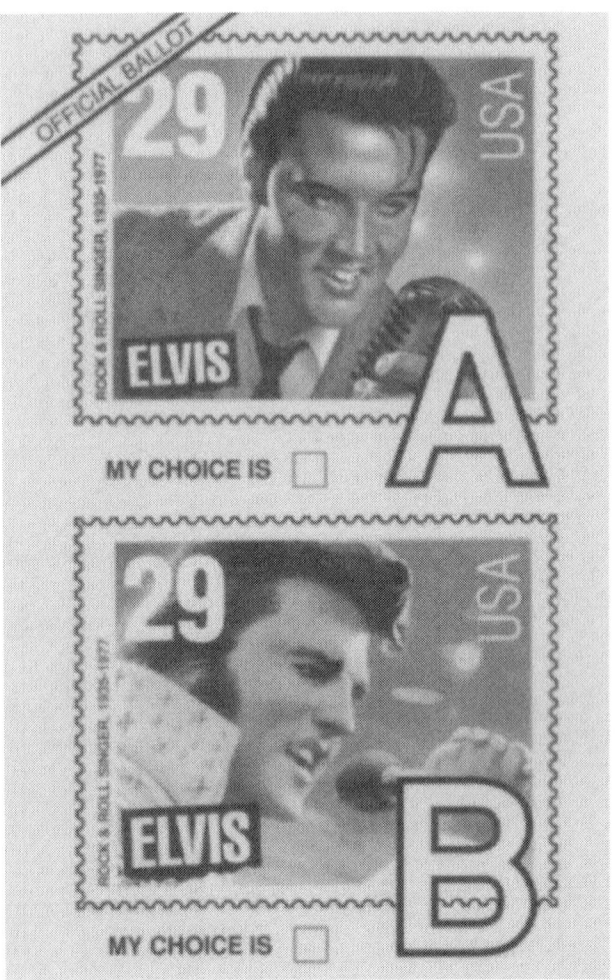

Elvis was always controversial, and this didn't change after decades of his passing. The icon's appearance on a stamp was heatedly debated in various cultural circles and even reached the congress.

A verdict was finally reached, Elvis was approved by the officials.

The Postal Services then had the brilliant idea of including the public in the design selection process.

A poster appeared overnight in every post office, and eventually, People magazine decided to feature it on its cover. The poster had two designs of <u>the Elvis stamp</u>; one when he was starting out and another at his prime.

The poster had a tagline that drove endless discussions later on: "Decide which Elvis is king." The stamp garnered staggering fame even before it was issued.

The people voted for 'Young Elvis'. That was back in 1992.

11. The First Commemorative Stamp

The first time stamps were used to commemorate a public figure was in 1893. The first commemorative stamp was part of the 400th-anniversary celebration of Christopher Columbus.

The stamp was issued at a 2-cent rate. It's based on a work of art featuring Columbus and his fleet. The engraving was made by Alfred Jones and Charles Skinner.

12. Self-Adhesive Stamps From Sierra Leone

The very first self-adhesive stamp saw the light of day in 1964. That was an innovative and bold decision from Sierra Leone. It had a green background and featured a map of the country.

The world of stamps had expected this to happen, but who'd take the first the first step wasn't very clear.

Stamp collectors have issues regarding the durability and life-expectancy of these stamps. Officials have concerns of their own about the paper procurement and processing logistics.

That's why this 'novelty' took its time and it's still not a fait-accompli!

13. Celebrity Stamp Collectors

Collecting stamps is one of the oldest hobbies known to man. It's not surprising to see numerous celebrities among these hobbyists.

Charlie Chaplin was an avid stamp collector, and so were Freddie mercury, Jacque Costeau, Ayn Rand, and Franklin Delano Roosevelt.

Currently, Maria Sharapova has let the public in on her passion for stamp collection. Patrick Dempsey shares her interest, as well as Nicolas Sarkozy, Warren Buffet, and Queen Elizabeth.

14. Bhutan's Music Stamp

A Brilliant Businessman was led by a series of adventures to the Kingdom of Bhutan. Burt Todd fell in love with that exotic land and two years later, returned back with his bride.

Todd was the ultimate Scientist-Maverick, and when he realized that Bhutan had financial difficulties, he offered to help.

His unorthodox contribution was unusual stamps. He created eye-catching designs to generate revenue. The most outlandish of them all was the 'Talking Stamp'. It was a mini-vinyl record that you could play on a regular turntable. That was in 1972.

15. A Stamp With an Ad on the Back

The clever ad-campaign stamp appeared in NewZealand, back in 1893. Postmaster-General Sir Joseph Ward thought it was a good idea to place a little ad on the back of stamps, and he went on full throttle!

The ads brought in plenty of cash to the postal service, but many users frowned upon it. The ink plus the adhesive made for an unsavory taste. People rarely used a sponge to moisten stamps, as you might know, the tongue was often an easier device. The printed ads stopped around 1895.

This comes to prove that you can find an ad anywhere, even on the back of a stamp!

16. Britain's First Christmas Stamp 1966

The first Royal Mail Christmas stamps were issued in 1966 using designs created by two six-year-old school children. The designs were selected after the post office organized a stamp-design competition for schoolchildren that attracted 5,000 entries.

The winning designs were the King of the Orient drawn by T Shemza that featured on the 3d stamp and a snowman drawn by J Berry that featured on the 1s 6d stamp. In a famous printing error one stamp on each sheet of the 3d design was missing the T in T Shemza's name and this error affectionately became known as the "Missing T" (SG 272c).

Save1966 Christmas 3d Albany Stamps1966 Christmas 3d

The competition was so popular that it was launched again in 1981. For those who remember the release of these first Christmas stamps in 1966 it is quite a thought that the six year olds that designed these stamps are now retirement age.

17. 1972 Ajman Stamp

In 1972, Ajman issued 1,773 stamps and 193 miniature sheets. Many of the stamps issued by Ajman were available perforate and imperforate. This is a colossal feat, to put it into perspective Great

Britain hadn't produced its 1,733rd stamp until 20 years later in 1993 and many countries have still not reached this number yet.

St Helena began issuing stamps in 1856 and after 150 years they had just passed the one thousand mark, leaving quite some way to go.

18. Austria's Innovative Stamps

When it comes to unique stamps there is one country that immediately comes to mind, Austria. Making stamps interesting, the innovative designers in Austria have created a far few head-turners that collectors love.

Utilizing all the techniques they could possibly use for a stamp, Austria has created an eclectic mix of designs including; porcelain stamps featuring the Viennese Rose, leather Lederhosen stamps created in cooperation with Swarowski featuring six Swarowski crystals and even a glass postage stamp featuring a glass painting of the Virgin Mary mourning over her son.

Another interesting stamp is an embroidered stamp featuring the Dirndl, a local Austrian outfit. The embroidered stamp is made into the shape of a Dirndl and features three colours.

19. Inverted Jenny Stamps of 1918

When it comes to stamp collecting, errors are celebrated and are extremely popular. One of the most popular stamp errors is known as the 'Inverted Jenny' and is an airmail stamp that features an upside-down airplane.

An unused, original 'Inverted Jenny' stamp is highly prized and is valued at hundreds of thousands of dollars. There are only around 100 Inverted Jenny stamps that still exist.

20. Perfins to Prevent Stamp Theft

During the 19th century, stealing stamps from offices was common among employees. The stamps could be used to send mail without charge and could even be used to pay for small purchases.

To stop this theft from happening companies began to perforate initials onto stamps as a way of marking ownership and preventing private use of the stamps. The perfin stamps could then be easily identified as stolen property and stores would refuse to accept them as payment.

Perfins were introduced in Britain in 1868 and in America in 1908.

21. The Barbuda Bird Stamps Decline in Value

Sometimes stamp designs skyrocket in value, other times they lose their value. It can be luck of the draw but many collectors bank on their stamps increasing in value over time.

There are stories of Stanley Gibbons pricing items very low when they didn't have them in stock and then raising the price considerably once they had built up stocks. Whether there is truth to this or not is unknown but the price of stamps doesn't always increase.

A key example is the 1976 Barbuda bird stamp set. In 1992 a set of 6 was catalogued at £20. Now, the same set is priced at just £1. Anyone who invested in these stamps may be left feeling a little blue over the decline in value.

22. Nigeria's 1961 Original Artwork Stamps

Sometimes original artwork stamps appear at auction, there is one very interesting piece that caught our attention.

Stamp Store On LineNigeria 1961 First Anniversary of Independence Fine Mint SG 106 Scott 118 Other Nigerian Stamps
The stamp size artwork is an essay for the proposed Nigeria 1961 definitive series produced by Waterlows. This particular piece was for

the 4d value and while this may not sound like much there are two things that truly make this piece remarkable:

- The artwork was created probably using a one-haired paintbrush on a 18mm x 22mm scale.
- The artist remains unknown.

Sometimes these fascinating pieces show up and this 1961 original artwork is definitely one of those that catches people's eyes and attention.

23. Biggest Stamp Collection in the World

Without a doubt one of the biggest collections by an individual was held by Alan Roy who spent 70 years collecting over 2 million stamps. Alan Roy worked as a postman and was passionate about collecting stamps, dedicating his life to building his substantial collection.

The largest collection of first day covers stamps was awarded to George Vavvas by the Guinness World Records in 2013. Mr Vavvas' collection is 7,215 strong with stamps from 119 different countries.

24. The "Forever Stamp"

In 2007 the United States launched a forever stamp, this stamp pictured the Liberty Bell and are always valid for the postage rate of a first-class (1 ounce) letter no matter how the stamp prices change.

This means no matter when it was bought or how much you paid for the forever stamp it can be used to send a first class letter.

The forever stamps will always have the value of the current first-class mail rate, this means when they were introduced they had the value of 41 cents and in 2009 it increased to 44 cents.

25. Smallest Stamp Ever

Stamps are already very small in size but there are some that were created even smaller!

The smallest stamp ever produced for actual postage was issued in 1863 in Bolivar in Colombia. The stamp was 8 x 9.5mm and featured the Coat of Arms of Bolivar.

These stamps are very rare and come in two versions, one features five stars and the other features six. These tiny stamps were a fraction of the standard American stamp which is 22.10mm x 24.89mm in size.

26. 10 Year Waiting Period for Commemorative Stamps

There is a customary 10 year waiting period between when a person dies and when they are allowed to appear on a commemorative stamp.

The only exception to this rule is dead presidents, stamps commemorating dead presidents can be released on the presidents first birthday following their death.

Problems in production meant that President Nixon's commemorative stamp was issued about five months later and around 160 Nixon stamps were misprinted with an off-center portrait and his name printed upside-down.

28. First Stamp to Picture an Animal

The first animals to appear on stamps were beavers and bears.

In 1845 St Louis Post Office issued a set of provincial stamps featuring two bears holding a heraldic disc. The stamps were known as the 'St. Louis Bears' and cost 5 and 10 cent.

The first stamp that featured an animal in a natural way was the Canada three pence stamp that featured a beaver on the bank of a flowing river. The threepenny beaver was issued in 1851 and was designed by Sir Sandford Flemming. This beaver stamp was also the Province of Canada's first issued postage stamp.

29. Most Self Adhesive Stamps are Vegetarian

Here's a fun fact that probably hasn't even crossed your mind before but now you know, you'll never forget… The glue on the back of stamps in vegetarian! According to the UK Royal Mail envelope and stamp adhesive is almost always vegan as no animal products are involved.

Oh, and if you lick a stamp it is about 1/10th of a calorie.

60 Million Stamp Collectors

We'll wrap up these facts with one that pays homage to the popularity of stamp collecting across the globe. In 2013, the Wall Street Journal estimated that the number of stamp collectors in the world was around 60 million.

It was also stated that at least a third of these collectors are in China, where the hobby is rapidly growing. An estimate for the number of stamp collectors in the United States sits at 20 million people.

Stamp collecting is fun, affordable and promotes connection not only to each other but also to history. Stamps have sentimental value and can be a financial investment too. Collections can be passed down through generations and bring people together. They are a small piece of history that people around the world enjoy collecting.

Conclusion

Stamps aren't just the fee people used to pay in exchange for a letter delivery service. Stamps tell stories.

Every person, place, symbol, or even surreal design, has an interesting reason for how it reached the face of the stamp.

Stamps have release dates but their journeys never end. People often gift their stamp collections to children, grandchildren, and friends.

The stamp keeps on changing hands, and maybe someone would ask: who's that face featured on this stamp? And why is he there?

They'll probably learn a fun fact as they search for the answer, and the story goes on.

The most expensive stamps in the world

When the first stamp was issued in 1840, few could have suspected that it would inspire a passion that would last for centuries. The only thing that has increased more than the historical significance of stamps is the amount of money stamp collectors can make from them. Our experts have curated a list of the most expensive **stamps** in the world, and explained why each is so valuable.

The Penny Black - €3,000 Issued in the United Kingdom in May 1840, the Penny Black was the first adhesive stamp in the world, which is why this stamp is considered so valuable. The Penny Black carries a picture of Queen Victoria II and does not show the country of origin, as is custom today. Despite there being plenty of Penny Blacks for sale, an unused one can earn a lucky owner around €3,000, making it a very popular amongst collectors.

The Penny Black was the first adhesive stamp

Inverted Swan - €35,500 The Inverted Swan is one of the most famous and unique stamps in the world, not because of its beauty, but rather because it was one of the first invert errors in the world. The Inverted Swan was issued in Perth, Australia in 1855, when a complicated process of producing these stamps through lithography was followed. However, contrary to popular belief, it is actually the frame that is inverted rather than the swan. This famous stamp was last sold in 1983 for €35,500.

The Inverted Swan is the first example of a valuable invert error

Red Mercury - €37,000 The Red Mercury stamp is extremely valuable due to its rarity. Rather than a postage stamp, the Red Mercury was used for mailing newspapers. These stamps possess an image of the Roman god and were printed in yellow, red and blue depending on a number of newspapers in the bundle. However, the Red Mercury was short-lived and was soon replaced, which is why so few copies have survived and why they hold such a high value of €37,000.

The Red Mercury stamp was used for delivering newspapers

Hawaiian Missionaries - €39,000 Despite the cheap blue paper that the Hawaiian Missionaries stamp was printed on, these are amongst the rarest and most valuable stamps of all time, now worth around €39,000. The Hawaiian Missionaries were the first stamps to be produced in Hawaii and were predominantly used in correspondence between missionaries, hence their name.

Despite the cheap paper, Hawaiian Missionaries stamps have become incredibly valuable

Inverted Dendermonde - €75,000 The Inverted Dendermonde, which showcases the town hall upside down, is **Belgium**'s greatest contribution to printing errors. Although this error leaked through two sheets of the stamp's first run and one pane of the second, only 17 are known to still exist. It is rumoured that two of these stamps were lost when a famous stamp collector was murdered in 1942. If you wanted to get your hands on the remaining few, it would set you back an estimated €75,000.

The Inverted Dendermonde may have been motivation for a murder in 1942

Inverted Jenny - €750,000 Another printing error is what placed the huge price tag on the Inverted Jenny. Now worth around €750,000, this stamp features an upside-down image of the Curtiss JN-4 airplane and was issued in the US in 1918. Only 100 copies managed to make it through printing, which is why the Inverted Jenny is valued so highly.

Only 100 copies of the Inverted Jenny were ever printed

Baden 9 Kreuzer - Around €1 Million Rather than being valuable for an image error, the Baden 9-Kreuzer takes its value from an error in the colour used. A 9-Kreuzer stamp has the face value of 9-Kreuzer and is colored pink, whilst the 6-Kreuzer stamps were green. However, an error in printing meant that a batch of 9-Kreuzer stamps was colored green, rather than pink. Only four are known to exist and one was sold in 2008 for over €1 million.

A green Baden 9-Kreuzer can reach a six figure sum at auction.

The First Two Mauritius - Over €1 Million Issued in 1847 in Mauritius during the British Colony, these stamps were modeled on the British stamps with an image of Queen Victoria. With only 26 known copies known to still exist and as the first **British Commonwealth Stamps** to be produced outside of Great Britain, it is no wonder that the Mauritius stamps hold a value of over €1

million each.

The first British Commonwealth Stamps to be produced outside Great Britain

The Treskilling Yellow - Over €2.1 Million The Treskilling Yellow is considered to be one of the most expensive postage stamps in the world, due to the fact instead of being printed in the usual colours (blue-green) it was actually printed in yellow. This Swedish misprinted stamp issued in 1855 is believed to be the only surviving copy to exist, which is why it is worth over €2.1 million. The stamp has been sold a few times and with each sale its value climbs.

Printed in Great Britain
by Amazon